The Bible On
The Temptations of Man

The Bible

on

The Temptations

of Man

by B. VAN IERSEL

Translated by F. Vander Heijden, O. Praem.

ST. NORBERT ABBEY PRESS
De Pere, Wisconsin
U. S. A.
1966

Nihil obstat:

　　　　　Samuel D. Jadin, O. Praem.
　　　　　Censor deputatus

Imprimatur:

　　　　　†Stanislaus V. Bona, D.D.
　　　　　Bishop of Green Bay
　　　　　March 5, 1966

© 1966 ST. NORBERT ABBEY PRESS

Originally published as
De Bijbel over Mensen in Bekoring
Roermond and Maaseik, J. J. Romen & Zonen, 1962

Library of Congress catalogue card number: 66 - 16991

Printed in the United States of America
ST. NORBERT ABBEY PRESS
De Pere, Wisconsin

CONTENTS

FOREWORD

When soil is to be analyzed to know its composition, no one expects all of it to be taken into the laboratory. It is sufficient to make a few test-borings to get the necessary samples. Analysis of these leads to conclusions of a general nature. In like manner, the biblical ground, on which the Christian lives, cannot be analyzed in its entirety. Nor does this matter. In Holy Scripture, too, test-borings can be made, through which the elementary structure comes to light.

In this book we have the results of such a test-boring. We hope that the sample which has come up will be of some value. It brings to light a point of special interest. The different chapters of this book have already appeared in **Het Heilig Land,** new series, 14 (1961) and 15 (1962). Chapter five, which treats the temptation of Christ, was written first. At its writing it became apparent that the situation which we indicate by the word "temptation" belongs to the essential structure of the human and Christian existence. When we looked further into the Old and the New Testament it also became apparent that this fundamental pattern was found in several other places as well, even though various interpretations were necessary. But this made this inquiry so intriguing.

If our readers will come to our conclusion that the situation of temptation has not only negative but also positive aspects, and that therefore there is no reason to fear it, we will deem the labor which produced this book richly compensated.

TRYING, TEMPTING, TESTING, ENTICING

When writing in a modern language about the Bible one continually encounters difficulties. The material was written in Hebrew and Greek. Its descriptions portray a totally different world of thinking and living. This greatly influences the vocabulary. In our language, for example, there are words for which no equivalent can be found in Hebrew and in Greek. And vice versa, Hebrew and Greek words may be translated into our language in different ways. In the process many associations are lost. The fields of semantics are entirely different.

This difficulty is especially felt when we study the biblical concept of temptation. In Hebrew we must start from the word **nasah,** in Greek from **peirazein.** At once there are a number of problems. These words place us in a sphere entirely different from our concept of the verb "to tempt." From tempting to enticing is but a step. In Hebrew and in Greek this is not true. In both languages we are much closer to the neutral verb "to try." In a number of texts this word means only "to attempt" (Deut. 4:34; 1 Sam. 17:39), "to make an effort" (Acts 9:26; 16:7;

24:6; 26:21). At times the meaning is to experiment or test. Thus Gideon makes a trial with his fleece (Judg. 6:39), the queen of Sheba comes to Jerusalem in order to test Solomon (1 Kings 10:1; 2 Chron. 9:1) and in Dan. 1:8-16 we find a description of the experiment to which Daniel and his associates submitted when they persistently refused to touch unclean food. Here we are really in the realm of the experiment. We see the same meaning when we are called upon to examine ourselves (Sirach 37:37; 2 Cor. 13:5) or to be careful about certain people as long as we are not experimentally sure that we can rely upon them (Sir. 6:7; 13:11; 27:5-7). Such an experiment can also take the form of persecution or torture as, for example, when the faith of the just is tested (Wisd. 2:17). Finally, the word may be used in such an extenuated meaning that it practically indicates only "to feel" (Wisd. 12:26).

We may ask ourselves whether it is worth while to point all this out. The answer must be affirmative. In this way the fundamental significance of the word is brought into sharper focus. Here we are concerned with a kind of test, a trial, by which we experimentally ascertain the condition of things. Moreover, this fundamental significance of "testing" is also understood whenever the word really means "enticing."

There may be some doubt about the best equivalent for these words. "Tempting" and "temptation" have a hereditary taint. They smack too much of enticing. The man who is said to be tempted is seen as standing too close to sin. "Trying" as well as "testing" would render the meaning very well, because these words have a strong connotation of experimentation. The noun "trial," on the other hand, is less expressive; this is used especially for calamities and hardships which befall us. "Visitation" is for many a Catholic a foreign word; to his ears it will probably sound a little "calvinistic" and perhaps remind him of what in Dutch is called "the language of Canaan," the language of the old-fashioned Bible translations. Still this word has its good aspects. Even though the meaning of experimentation is hardly implied, the word is in any case general enough to allow several meanings. The verb "to visit" cannot be used, because this is almost exclusively used in the meaning of calling upon someone. A visit is something quite different from a visitation.

Therefore in this book we have had to compromise without — we hope — compromising ourselves. For several reasons we have preferred the word "tempting." The chief reason is that this word — especially in the Catholic vocabulary — is still sufficiently open to allow the different meanings of the original Hebrew and Greek to be understood. The reader should know that whenever we use "enticing," "trying," or like words, the original text always uses one and the same word. For the titles of the different chapters we have purposely chosen different words to fit the subject.

THE TRIAL OF ABRAHAM

In the life of every man there are many temptations, trials, visitations. Nevertheless, only the very critical moments are especially and directly recognized as such. Lesser ones are recognized only later. When David saw Bethsheba bathing on the roof of a neighboring house he probably had no idea to what this scene would lead him. Only later will it have become clear to him what a severe trial this really had been. Likewise the old Israel recognizes the story of Abraham as a trial and it gives form to this insight from the way in which the story is told. Thus we read in Gen. 22:1-19:

"After these things God tested Abraham, and said to him: Abraham! And he said: Here am I. He said: Take your son, your only son Isaac, whom you love, and go to the land of Moriah, and offer him there as a burnt offering upon one of the mountains of which I shall tell you. So Abraham rose early in the morning, saddled his ass, and took two of his young men with him, and his son Isaac, and he cut the wood for the burnt offering, and arose and went to the place of which God had told him. On the third day Abraham lifted up his eyes and saw the place

afar off. Then Abraham said to his young men: Stay
here with the ass; I and the lad will go yonder and
worship, and come again to you. And Abraham took
the wood of the burnt offering, and laid it on Isaac
his son; and he took in his hand the fire and the
knife. So they went both of them together. And
Isaac said to his father Abraham: My father! And he
said: Here am I, my son. He said: Behold, the fire
and the wood; but where is the lamb for a burnt
offering? Abraham said: God will himself provide
the lamb for a burnt offering, my son. So they went
both of them together.

When they came to the place of which God had
told him, Abraham built an altar there, and laid the
wood in order, and bound Isaac his son, and laid
him on the altar, upon the wood. Then Abraham
put forth his hand, and took the knife to slay his
son. But the angel of the Lord called to him from
heaven, and said: Abraham, Abraham! And he said:
Here am I. He said: Do not lay your hand on the
lad or do anything to him; for now I know that you
fear God, seeing you have not withheld your son,
your only son, from me. And Abraham lifted up his
eyes and looked, and behold, behind him was a ram,
caught in a thicket by his horns; and Abraham went
and took the ram, and offered it up as a burnt offering instead of his son. So Abraham called the name
of the place the Lord will provide, as it is said to
this day: On the mount of the Lord it shall be provided.

And the angel of Yahweh called to Abraham a

second time from heaven, and said: By myself I
have sworn, says the Lord, because you have done
this, and have not withheld your son, your only son,
I will indeed bless you, and I will multiply your
descendants as the stars of heaven and as the sand
which is on the seashore. And your descendants
shall possess the gate of their enemies, and by your
descendants shall all the nations of the earth bless
themselves, because you have obeyed my voice.
So Abraham returned to his young men, and they
arose and went together to Beersheba; and Abraham
dwelt at Beersheba."

This story is considered one of the masterpieces of
world literature. Each rereading makes a newer and
deeper impression. It is written without a single
trace of sentimentality. No emotions are mentioned
or indicated. Although the reader knows that God
was only trying Abraham and would not allow the
story to come to its fatal end, yet he feels deeply
concerned with father and son. We can point out
descriptive details, such as the stress put in verse 2
on the fact that Isaac is an only son, and the mention
in verse 6 that Abraham himself carries the fire
and the knife, two dangerous things, while Isaac
carries the wood; we can see the curious tempo,
very fast in the beginning (verses 1-5), delayed in
verses 5-8, and finshed in verses 9-10 in a close-up of
Abraham's posture, lifting the knife.

But this does not concern us. Our main regard is
the trial. Therefore we must concentrate on God

and Abraham. First we ought to look more closely at the whole passage.

Retouchings

We will notice that the text resembles a retouched photo. Features which did not show clearly enough have been touched up and those things which disfigured the photo have been eliminated. To one who knows the subject in question retouchings are easily discernible. In our case too they are not done so cunningly that they cannot be discovered.

This is the case with verses 15-18, which contain the oft repeated promise (Gen. 12:2-3; 13:15-17; 16:10; 17:1-17; 26:3-5, 24; 28:13-15; 35:11-12), modified in such a way that the formula is adapted to the story. These words are not new. The last part of verse 16 is taken literally from verse 12, and the last part of verse 18 typifies the fundamental attitude of Abraham and is repeated in 26:5. It therefore seems sufficiently clear, that we have here a case where something is added to the original story to adapt it to the general trend of the Abraham stories. We might say that a special traditional feature of the image of Abraham is emphasized, lest the reader fail to notice it.

There is another detail in which we can see a case of retouching, namely, the appearance of the angel of Yahweh. It is remarkable that this angel speaks as if he were God himself: in verse 12 "now I know" and "you have not withheld your son, your only son." It seems probable that in the original story there appeared no angel of Yahweh but the voice of Yahweh himself was heard from heaven. This retouching was made in the period when Israel believed that immediate contact of God with the world was unthinkable because of the incomparable divine majesty. This was not difficult. In verse 11 only the "angel" had to be inserted; but because of this there arose a certain irregularity in the text, which now can help us find the original text.

We need not consider the promise of verses 15-18, nor is it necessary to attribute any special significance to the intervention of the "angel of Yahweh." So, only the three leading characters are left: God, Abraham and Isaac.

Abraham and Isaac

Starting with Isaac we see clearly that the story obviously has more than one function. Although the chief characters are God and Abraham, Isaac certainly is not a supernumerary figure, as are the two servants who accompanied them on a great part of the journey. Isaac is Abraham's first born and at the same time his only son, as is significantly stressed in verses 2, 12. Later we will discuss the only son. Let us now direct our attention to the first born.

Sacrificing a first born to God is something which evokes few associations for us. With Israel it has real significance. The first fruits of the fields and of the womb belong entirely to Yahweh, because it is he who gives fertility. Therefore the firstlings of crops and animals are offered to him. The first son, "who opens the womb" belongs to him as well. In Israel however there can be no question of actually sacrificing children to Yahweh. If children were sometimes sacrified it was because people adapted themselves improperly to the religious customs of the Canaanites. The orthodox people knew very well that Yahweh did not demand human sacrifice; he abhorred it. Instead of the first born of the womb of women therefore they offered animals. The children were then considered "redeemed."

It seems to me that when the Israelites read this story they were not only reminded of this sacrifice of the firstborn, but that they interpreted it as a rejection of child-sacrifice. Possibly they considered this event of Abraham as the foundation for this rejection. It is not without reason that in Hebrew the book is called "In the beginning." In it general human conditions and defects are explained by pointing out what happened in the beginning. This is also the explanation for certain religious customs, as circumcision (Gen. 17): we are referred to the beginning. For all general human events an explanation was sought in the very beginning, in the creation and in the conduct of the first parents. For customs peculiar to Israel itself an explanation is sought in the time of the patriarchs of Israel. So also as people in Israel read this story they were reminded of the command of the Law (i.e. of God himself), that Yahweh forbids the firstborn to be sacrificed to him, even though they belonged to him as much as the firstlings of fruits and animals.

The story has still another function. As we know, we find in Genesis a great number of popular etymologies of the names of persons (3:20; 4:25; 19: 37-38; 21:6, 17; 25:26-27; 29:31-35; 30:6-13, 18-24; 35:10, 18; 28:29-30) and places (11:9; 16:14; 26:33; 28:19; 31:47; 32:31). We find such an explanation here also, namely, the name of the mount in verse 14. In what way this name is part of the oldest tradition we need not consider. Perhaps there was a place with such a name where the sacrificing of rams instead of a firstborn was common. It is remarkable however that a place with such a name cannot be identified; also that the mountain in the land of the Moriah cannot be pointed out more precisely. That this is identical with the mountain on which Jerusalem was built is a later tradition and cannot be proved. This tradition supposes a connection between the sacrifices in the temple and the ram which Abraham offered in place of Isaac.

Abraham and God

But Isaac is not the chief character of the story, which is not part of the Isaac-cycle but rather of the Abraham-cycle. The narrative centers around Abraham and Yahweh and it is here that we find its chief concern. Yahweh wishes to test Abraham, and Abraham undergoes this test in a splendid manner. He obeys the incredible order of Yahweh without hesitation. The story tells us this much, and this is the image of Abraham in the minds of his children. What is strange in it is not so much the fact that Yahweh asks him to surrender his dearest possession: only the best of one's possessions must be offered to Yahweh, and it must be without blemish or stain. Only the best is good enough. Moreover, Israel was always aware that some peoples offered their children to their gods and that this custom — however much it contradicted Israel's faith — was also followed in Palestine itself during certain periods. The order of Yahweh therefore would seem less incomprehensible to an old Israelite than to us.

There is however a quite different aspect. Verse 2 stresses not only that Isaac was Abraham's beloved son, but his only one. This changes the situation and has far reaching consequences, especially in the case of Abraham. Isaac is the only link between Abraham and the progeny which had been promised him (12:2; 13:16; 14:5; 17:4-6). Without this link fulfillment of the promise becomes impossible. It seems as if Yahweh, who made possible the fulfillment of the promise by giving a son to the barren Sarah (Gen. 21) takes away what he has given and therefore withdraws his promise.

The letter to the Hebrews points to this when it places the portrait of Abraham in the gallery of the fathers of the faith (Hebr. 11) and says of him: "By faith Abraham, when he was tested, offered up Isaac, and he who had received the promises was ready to offer up his only son, of whom it was said: Through Isaac shall your descendants be named. He considered that God was able to raise men even from the dead; hence, figuratively speaking, he did receive him back" (Heb. 11:17-19).

Whether Abraham's faith went as far as Hebrews supposes is a question we need not answer. Undoubtedly the fact that Isaac was a necessary link in the fulfillment of the promise must be considered as something which made the trial of Abraham a kind of dilemma: to obey means to make impossible the fulfillment of the promise; to refuse means to be unfaithful to Yahweh, who is to fulfill the promise.

The reader knows from the beginning (verse 1) that this is only a test, but it is also evident that it was not so for Abraham. A voice from heaven tells him this later (verse 12). The situation is indeed as the letter to the Hebrews says in the above quoted text: Abraham did offer the sacrifice of Isaac, even though Yahweh prevented the outcome. The journey of three days which began the day that Abraham heard God's demand is probably mentioned (verses 2-3) to make it clear that Abraham's obedience was not a passing emotion. It was firm willingness. Rightly therefore Sirach can write that Abraham was found faithful in this trial (Sir. 44:20).

God and man

The story becomes more problematic only when we direct our attention to God who also plays an important part. He asks Abraham to sacrifice Isaac. In itself this is not objectionable. The author tells his story in such a way that we know at the outset that this demand was not real. It was only a test. Now questions arise. God does lead Abraham into temptation. What was his purpose? Of course not that

Abraham through this temptation would fall into disobedience and thus into sin. This could not be God's
purpose. But he does bring Abraham into a situation
in which he could just as well choose disobedience
as obedience. We may feel inclined to take into
account that God knew that Abraham would prove
faithful. But this is no solution, because the author
evidently thinks otherwise. This we see in verse 12:
"Do not lay your hand on the lad or do anything to
him; for now I know that you fear God, seeing you
have not withheld your son, your only son, from
me." The story really supposes that God did not
know the result beforehand and that it was exactly
by means of this trial that he wished to find out.
Yahweh wants to know what Abraham really is like
and to this end he leads him into temptation: into a
critical situation, in which Abraham is forced to
make an extreme, and therefore decisive, choice.
From this choice God can conclude whether or not
Abraham is faithful to him.

We need not mention that for us this is unaccept-
able. This type of thinking is clearly corrected in
the New Testament. "Let no one say when he is
tempted: I am tempted by God; for God cannot be
tempted with evil and he himself tempts no one; but
each person is tempted when he is lured and enticed
by his own desire" (Jas. 1:13-14). This is very clear
language; so it seems at least. The reality is less
clear than it appears. It is evident that James is
thinking first of all of a temptation directed toward
sin. Indeed, God cannot tempt us to sin. Nor was

this the case with Abraham. Yet the author says
God did put Abraham to the test in order to know
what he would do. Actually this is a very primitive
method of expression. God is pictured here in a
very anthropomorphic way. For man it is necessary
to try things, handle them, be occupied with them
in order to know what they are like. But the psalmist
already knew, that this was certainly not the case
with God. God looks into the hearts of men (Ps.
11:4), he knows their thoughts (Ps. 94:1-2), their
intentions (Ps. 139:1-4), their secret plans (Ps. 44:2
and 139:2), not only at this moment but also in the
future. He is not in need of any experience with
man. It is not necessary that he test man or try him
in certain situations, as is described in this story.
This is a detail which on the one hand shows us
that this story dates back to early times when
Israel still had primitive opinions about its God.
But on the other hand it is less acceptable to us.
What are we to do with an idea about God which
has been known to be wrong for centuries? God
does not need experiments. Should we therefore
consider this description of Yahweh testing Abraham
as a very primitive vision, which was later dropped
by Israel and a fortiori by ourselves? Should we
just point to the letter of James 1:13-14 and say
that God in no way has anything to do with this
experiment, which was such a great temptation for
Abraham? Perhaps it is wise to withhold our judg-
ment until the time when we have studied other
texts where there is question of trials. Perhaps we
will then see some light.

3

YAHWEH AND HIS PEOPLE

It is with good reason that the old Israel has kept in its holy books a tradition which describes for us its patriarch as a man tried by God. There are several reasons for this. Without a doubt one reason was the fact that Israel recognized its own experiences in these events and understood its own situations in them. This in concrete terms means: Israel too has been in situations in which the people, under the influence of pagan surroundings, sacrificed children. The law and the prophets rejected this. They knew better therefore, but they succumbed to the temptation; they actually bowed not before Yahweh but before idols.

The time of trial

Not all periods in a man's life are equally crowded with experiences. After all, life has its rhythm. This is also true of trials and temptations, which are more numerous and stronger at one time than another. In the memory of the old Israel there is also one period remembered especially as a time of divine trials. This does not mean that there were not serious trials at other times. We need think only of the stay in Egypt, of settlement in Canaan, when pagan influences were so strong, or of the time of exile, when they came into very close contact with other gods and other customs in Babylon, or of the second century B.C., when adaptation to the practices and ideas of the Greek world threatened to destroy Israel.

In these periods trials very often came in the form of persecutions. Especially is this true in the last two centuries before Christianity. Therefore it was not just accidental that in these days suffering was called a trial to which God subjected the just in order to test them (see Wisd. chap. 2-3, especially 3:5-6; Tob. 12:13; Sirach 4:17).

The conviction that suffering and persecution were part of the trial ordained by God plays an important role. The words of Judith in the book of this name are a clear example:

"For if we are captured all Judea will be captured and our sanctuary will be plundered; and he will exact of us the penalty for its desecration. And the slaughter of our brethren and the captivity of the land and the desolation of our inheritance — all this he will bring upon our heads among the Gentiles, wherever we serve as slaves; and we shall be an offense and a reproach in the eyes of those who acquire us. For our slavery will not bring us into favor, but the Lord our God will turn it to dishonor.

Now therefore, brethren, let us set an example to our brethren, for their lives depend upon us, and

the sanctuary and the temple and the altar rest upon
us. In spite of everything let us give thanks to the
Lord our God, who is putting us to the test as he
did our forefathers. Remember what he did with
Abraham, and how he tested Isaac, and what happened to Jacob in Mesopotamia in Syria, while he
was keeping the sheep of Laban, his mother's brother.
For he has not tried us with fire, as he did them, to
search their hearts, nor has he taken revenge upon
us; but the Lord scourges those who draw near to
him, in order to admonish them" (Jud. 8:21-27).

The time however which Israel considered especially a time of trial is the period of forty years
in the desert, when God led his people out of Egypt,
the house of slavery. In Exodus 16 we see how
Yahweh tried his people. We read here that Israel,
no longer accustomed to the hardships of life in
the desert, grumbled against Moses and made remarks
that the fleshpots of Egypt were to be preferred to
the desert where one went hungry. Yahweh himself,
who in the strength of his mighty arm led his people
from the slavery of Egypt, helps them and supplies
their needs by giving them the mysterious manna.

At the same time he tries Israel to see whether or
not they will live according to his law, by demanding
that on the day before the sabbath they collect food
for two days, and not collect any on the day of rest.
This aspect of the journey through the desert is
described in a more detailed way in Deut. 8:2-6:
"And you shall remember all the way which Yahweh
your God has led you these forty years in the

wilderness, that he might humble you testing you to know what was in your heart, whether you would keep his commandments, or not. And he humbled you and let you hunger and fed you with manna, which you did not know, nor did your fathers know; that he might make you know that man does not live by bread alone, but that man lives by everything that proceeds out of the mouth of the Lord. Your clothing did not wear out upon you, and your foot did not swell, these forty years. Know then in your heart that, as a man disciplines his son, the Lord your God disciplines you. So you shall keep the commandments of the Lord your God, by walking in his ways and by fearing him."

This is a valuable text. Some particulars deserve attention. God himself imposed the trial in the difficult situation in the desert. Israel is forced to a definite decision. Exodus 16 clearly describes how some of the people went out on the sabbath to collect the manna, although the majority evidently kept God's law. The situation forces everyone to make a choice. This is what God wills.

Deut. 8:2-6 makes it plain that God insists on knowing what his people are like. Therefore it is necessary that the road toward unfaithfulness to his commands should lie open to them. Only then can he — thus Deuteronomy tells us — know the mind of his people, whether or not they are truly prepared to obey.

We take a different view when we do not see

temptation as a test, an experimental situation, a critical moment in which believing man receives the opportunity to show the depth of his faith by making a conscious choice for that which is or is not willed by God. If we see a trial chiefly as an enticement to sin we cannot ascribe it to God.

Satan

In 2 Chron. 32:31 it is still Yahweh who tries king Hezekiah and the praying faithful in Psalm 26:2; Sirach 31:10 still asks God to try him. It is different in the book of Job. Consider especially the foreword in the first and second chapters. Here we have the heavenly prelude to Job's trials, where it is evident that it is not Yahweh himself who tries Job by the calamities and accidents which befall him. On the contrary this happens through one of the members of the heavenly court, which consists of the "sons of God." From the narrative we get a strong impression that it is these sons of God who maintain relations between God and the world. They report to him the things which happen there and execute his orders. Elsewhere they are called God's delegates or messengers or the angel of Yahweh. The reason it was deemed necessary to place such beings between God and man perhaps lies in the fact that they considered Yahweh to be too exalted to occupy himself personally with these things.

Now one of the members of God's court is **"the satan."** The article shows that this is a function, which we may compare to that of a public prose-cutor (Ps. 109:6). Thus "**the satan**" in the heavenly tribunal is the prosecutor of man, and as such he proposes to try Job, because his virtuous life does not seem to be real: Job's piety goes hand in hand with great wealth. **The satan** thinks that this piety will not remain in less fortunate circumstances. It is this **satan** who bring calamities to Job.

We are inclined to think here of the devil. This does not seem probable. Although the satan is described in such a way as if he evidently would like Job to fall into sin, he is in fact a member of the heavenly court and stands before God's throne as one of God's sons. We may ask ourselves whether the trials of Job must not, after all, be ascribed to God. It seems that the reason the satan was placed between God and Job, is not that the author thinks that God himself could not place Job in such a painful test-situation, but because he believes that such a heavenly being should be placed between God and man.

Nevertheless the presence of this heavenly satan may be the beginning of a new viewpoint. We have another text (Zech. 3:1 ff.) in which the satan is near the angel of Yahweh to accuse the high priest Joshua; the accusation proves false. The angel of Yahweh calls God's punishment down upon the satan. Does this satan still reside in heaven? It is not certain; this is a vision of Zechariah, and is not localized in heaven or on earth.

A change occured in their thinking. This is evident from another text, 1 Chron. 21:1. The author of these books (300 B.C.) rewrote Israel's history. If we wish to see clearly the evolution which took place in the opinions prevalent in Israel, it is extremely useful to compare Samuel and Kings to 1 and 2 Chronicles. In many cases the only difference is a slight retouching of the old text. It is exactly these retouchings which give us an insight into the change which occurred in their opinions.

In 1 Chron. 21:1 we read that the census organized by king David was considered a great sin. We read in 2 Sam. 24:1: "Again the anger of the Lord was kindled against Israel, and he incited David against them, saying: Go, number Israel and Judah." Evidently here the description suggests that it is Yahweh himself who orders David to do something which he considers sinful and for which the people will later be punished. Here is a very primitive concept that Yahweh wishes everything on earth to happen as it does (see also the plagues of Egypt and the fact that Yahweh hardens the heart of the Pharaoh), a notion which was changed before the last book of the Old Testament was written. We see this change clearly in 1 Chron. 21:1, where we read: "Satan stood up against Israel, and incited David to number Israel."

The author of Chronicles has another interpretation: it is not Yahweh who entices David to this sin, but satan. The word is used here without its article. It evidently has become a proper name. There is

no mention who satan is. We get the impression
however that he is no longer a member of the
heavenly court, but God's adversary, who strives to
entice man into sin. He is the great tempter, who
does not intend to bring about a test-situation in
which man can realize his own faith, but who wishes
exclusively to make man sin. When we look only
at this aspect of the temptation, we can see it in
only one way. It is evident that this is a narrower
view of temptation than the concept which forms
the background of the above quoted texts of Scripture, where it is God himself who brings Israel
into temptation "that by them I may test Israel,
whether they will take care to walk in the way
of Yahweh as their fathers did, or not" (Judg. 2:22;
3:1, 4).

The people put God to the test

When speaking about the temptations which be-
fell Israel we should remember that there was
another which shows the reverse of the coin (Exodus:
17). Israel is not only tried by Yahweh; the people
in turn put Yahweh to the test. In this way the time
of the journey through the desert was remembered
by Israel not only as a period in which the people
were tested by Yahweh, but also as a time in which
they themselves challenged him. In Psalm 78, where
the sins of the forefathers are described, it is repeated
three times that they put God to the test (verses 18,
41 and 58; cf. also Ps. 106:14). Num. 14:23 says that
no one of the generation which wandered in the
desert shall be allowed to enter the promised land,

because they had put Yahweh to the test for the tenth time and refused to listen to his voice.

In several texts a specific place is mentioned in regard to this testing by God. Thus we read in Ps. 95:7-8: "Oh that today you would hearken to his voice. Harden not your hearts, as at Meribah, as on the day at Massah in the wilderness" (cf. also Deut. 6:16). The names "Massah" and "Meribah" are explained respectively as meaning "temptation" and "quarrel." Although we meet the name of Meribah alone in a number of texts, there are others where we always find the two names together; such is the remarkable text from the blessing of Moses: "Give to Levi thy Thummim, and thy Urim to thy godly one, whom thou didst test at Massah, with whom thou didst strive at the waters of Meribah" (Deut. 33:8). What is most remarkable in this text is not merely that the name Massah is connected with temptation; it also mentions that God put his favorite to the test. This is the opposite of what we find in the other texts! There are a number of problems here, with which we cannot occupy ourselves. Our only purpose is to make it evident that the name of this place in the desert was connected with a certain tradition which usually (i.e. except in the above quoted text) says that the people put Yahweh to the test in this place.

God in a forced position

This tradition is not described as extensively anywhere as in Exodus 17:1-7 where we read: "All of the congregation of the people of Israel moved on from the wilderness of sin by stages, according to the commandment of the Lord, and camped at Rephidim; but there was no water for the people to drink. Therefore the people found fault with Moses, and said: Give us water to drink. And Moses said to them: Why do you find fault with me? Why do you put the Lord to the proof? But the people thirsted there for water, and the people murmured against Moses, and said: Why did you bring us up out of Egypt, to kill us and our children and our cattle with thirst? So Moses cried to the Lord: What shall I do with this people? They are almost ready to stone me. And the Lord said to Moses: Pass on before the people, taking with you some of the elders of Israel, and take in your hand the rod with which you struck the Nile, and go. Behold, I will stand before you there on the rock at Horeb; and you shall strike the rock, and water shall come out of it, that the people may drink. And Moses did so, in the sight of the elders of Israel. And he called the name of the place Massah and Meribah, because of the fault-finding of the children of Israel, and because they put the Lord to the proof by saying: Is the Lord among us or not?"

This passage is related to Ex. 16, because in both cases trials are mentioned and both chapters show how Yahweh provided the Israelites in the desert with everything needed for sustenance. What we want to know is: What is the meaning of "Israel puts Yahweh to the test?" This expression really has a broader meaning and is used for numerous cases where Israel was unfaithful to Yahweh. Perhaps the real meaning can be more carefully indicated. Let us remember that Scripture here uses the same word for two different situations: God putting man to the test, and man putting God to the test. This suggests that the two situations have something in common. In both cases we have what might be called a forced position. The one case is a situation in which man is forced to prove that he will be true to his choice. The second case is a situation in which man tries to force God to show that he will be faithful to his given word. They try to force Yahweh's hand: he must do what they want of him, or they will renounce their faith. We find something similar in Exodus 17. Yahweh has to show that he accompanies his people and he must show this by providing water. If he does not do this, they will no longer believe that he is with them.

That this interpretation is correct can be shown from a text which is entirely different: Judith 8:10-13. Uzziah, the ruler of the town of Bethulia, which was beseiged and could not be held, wants to wait for five days before surrendering the town. If within that time God does not help, the town will be surrendered. Judith replies with the following words: "Listen to me, rulers of the people of Bethulia! What you have said to the people today is not right; you have even sworn and pronounced this oath between God and you, promising to surrender the city to our enemies unless the Lord turns and helps us within so many days. Who are you, that have put God to the test this day, and are setting

yourselves up in the place of God among the sons
of men? You are putting the Lord almighty to the
test — but you will never know anything." It is not
accidental that this situation is similar to Exodus
17. In both cases God's hand is being forced. He
must comply with what is desired of him. In both
cases they demand proof that God is with his people;
they demand signs. Because of this blackmailing,
this demanding sign as a condition for their confidence in Yahweh, their faith in him is being
destroyed. They treat God as a man, who must
prove his worth and must show that he is as good
as his word.

This thinking is not seen so clearly in all places.
The expression "putting God to the test" is often
used in a weaker sense. It may even mean almost
the opposite, as in the case of Achaz. He refuses
to ask a sign which Yahweh offers him and the
prophet Isaiah reproaches him that by his refusal
he puts God's patience to the test (Is. 7:10-16). But
the meaning underlying this expression when used
in a looser sense seems to be the same as we have
described. This is confirmed by the first verses of
the book of Wisdom: "Love righteousness, you
rulers of the earth, think of the Lord with upright-
ness, and seek him with sincerity of heart; because
he is found by those who do not put him to the test,
and manifests himself to those who do not distrust
him. For perverse thoughts separate men from
God, and when his power is tested, it convicts the
foolish" (1:1-3).

4

MAN SEDUCED

Gen. 2:8; 3:15

We can subscribe to the statement that Yahweh has led his people into temptation only as long as we see temptation not as a seduction to sin, but as a test-situation, where man is given an opportunity to realize his hidden possibilities for good and for evil, and by repeated choice, prove faithful to the proper choice. Moreover, we can subscribe to it only if we do not place God in an unapproachable heaven, from which he can have contact with man only by means of special messengers. With any other interpretation, there is no possibility of seeing God as the one who leads his people into temptation. In that case there is a intermediary, an angel or a devil, between God and man, who mediates between Yahweh and his people.

We find such a one whenever Israel's prophets and sages reflect on the situation of mankind. Evidently they are convinced that temptation is fundamental to the pattern of human existence. In the first chapters of Genesis, where they wrote the ground rules of human existence and human life, temptation plays an important role. Here it is not

God who leads man into temptation, but a mysterious snake. It is not that they think God so highly exalted above man that direct and immediate contact would be impossible: after the sin we see God walking in the garden (3:8) and talking with man (3:9). There must be another reason. Not only is man tried, but — and this changes the situation — he falls. This makes the trial a real temptation or even a seduction. Nevertheless, Yahweh does play a role here. It is he who has created this possibility of falling, by creating in the surroundings in which man lives, a situation which forces him to make a choice. The way God made man, man is not complete. God's creation is not an end, but a beginning. He leaves possibilities, so that man himself may realize them for good (and for evil!) (2:15-17).

Let us first read the passage in question, not considering that it deals with one definite man, called Adam, who lived in very ancient times, but with every man. Here we find a description of the fundamental pattern of all temptation.

"And the Lord God planted a garden in Eden, in the east; and there he put the man whom he had formed. And out of the ground the Lord God made to grow every tree that is pleasant to the sight and good for food, the tree of life also in the midst of the garden, and the tree of knowledge of good and evil . . . the Lord God took the man and put him in the garden of Eden to till it and keep it. And the Lord God commanded the man, saying: You may freely eat of every tree of the garden; but of the

tree of the knowledge of good and evil you shall
not eat, for in the day that you eat of it you shall
die . . .

Now the serpent was more subtle than any other
wild creature that the Lord God has made. He said
to the woman: Did God say: You shall not eat of
any tree of the garden? And the woman said to the
serpent: We may eat of the fruit of the trees of the
garden; but God said: You shall not eat of the fruit
of the tree which is in the midst of the garden,
neither shall you touch it, lest you die. But the
serpent said to the woman: You will not die. For
God knows that when you eat of it your eyes will be
opened, and you will be like God, knowing good
and evil. So when the woman saw that the tree
was good for food, and that it was a delight to the
eyes, and that the tree was to be desired to make
one wise, she took of its fruit and ate; and she also
gave some to her husband, and he ate. Then the
eyes of both were opened, and they knew that they
were naked; and they sewed fig leaves together and
made themselves aprons.

And they heard the sound of the Lord God
walking in the garden in the cool of the day, and the
man and his wife hid themselves from the presence
of the Lord God among the trees of the garden. But
the Lord God called to the man, and said to him:
Where are you? And he said: I heard the sound
of thee in the garden, and I was afraid, because I
was naked; and I hid myself. He said: Who told you
that you were naked? Have you eaten of the tree

of which I commanded you not to eat? The man said: The woman whom thou gavest to be with me, she gave me fruit of the tree, and I ate. Then the Lord God said to the woman: What is this that you have done? The woman said: The serpent beguiled me, and I ate. The Lord God said to the serpent: Because you have done this, cursed are you above all cattle, and above all wild animals; upon your belly you shall go, and dust you shall eat all the days of your life. I will put enmity between you and the woman, and between you and her seed; he shall bruise your head, and you shall bruise his heel" (Gen. 2:8; 3:15).

Man tempted

We cannot attempt to answer the many questions arising from this passage, for example, why the author speaks about a tree, the fruit of which man is not allowed to eat, why this tree is called the tree of knowledge of good and evil, why the seducer is pictured as a serpent etc. We will consider only what the text says about man being tempted.

It is noteworthy that the word "temptation" is not used. Nevertheless the passage aims to show how man comes to sin. There are many factors concerned. First of all there is the situation. God places man in a paradise full of trees, the fruits of which not only delight the eye but the tongue as well. The woman noticed that the "tree of knowledge of good and evil" was no exception. The appearance of its fruits evidently manifested a special delectability. However this tree is forbidden to man. He is not allowed to eat of it, because if he does he will die (it is not said that death would be a **punishment** for eating these fruits). It is not standing in a remote corner of the garden, but in the very middle of it. This detail has significance, because it gives us the impression that the whole garden is arranged around this tree. Man cannot avoid it, because he not only has to guard the garden but also to tend it. The situation therefore is really a temptation and a trial, because the circumstances make it a continuous "proximate occasion of sin," which man cannot escape. The description of the garden centers around the forbidden tree, but there are other items which play a role. We may consider these a literary device, by which the author prepares the reader for the fall. Nevertheless almost all circumstances correspond to common experience in which a temptation lurks; this aspect fascinates us because everything seems to contribute to the idea that the forbidden fruit should be as beautiful and attractive as possible.

This is the fundamental pattern of temptation, as is evident from the qualities of the fruit enumerated in 3:6. Perhaps (but this may be unwarranted psychological theorizing) we can say the same about what we read in 3:3: if one is forced to be on its defensive, the danger of falling is exaggerated, the forbidden area is extended beyond reality to create a safe margin. The woman says that it is forbidden even to touch the tree, because even this would cause them to die; but we read nothing about this in verse 2:17 where the tree is described. Man himself exaggerates the situation in which he has been placed by God.

But it is exactly this being on the defensive which makes man liable to falling. His equilibrium is no longer intact. A little push is sufficient to make him lose his balance and fall. When falling we have the impression that the final little push comes from without. This we see here too. Man is brought to his fall by his wife and his wife by the snake. Why this should be a snake we need not consider. In the text itself there is no reason to suppose the satan is hidden in the snake; that the seducer is inimical to God is not mentioned either. Perhaps we can suppose this attitude because of the role the snake plays in old eastern traditions. We may remark that neither the woman nor the man was aware of this design. The snake succeeds in convincing them that eating the forbidden fruit will have some good consequences for them. We see therefore that man, after the fall, when called upon by Yahweh to give a reckoning, rejects his own guilt. When Yahweh asks: Have you eaten of the tree of which I commanded you not to eat? The man answers: "The woman thou gavest to be with me, she gave me fruit of the tree, and I ate," and the woman in her turn passes the responsibility on to somebody else: "The serpent beguiled me, and I ate" (3:11-13). Nevertheless, not only the serpent (3:14-15) but also the woman (3:16) and man (3:17-19) are punished.

Always tempted

In the story of the fall we have a full portrait

of man being tempted. This succinct description relates the essentials of every temptation. The attractiveness of the forbidden road (3:6) always plays an important part, and it may so preoccupy us that we are forced to take an attitude of defense; this renders us extremely vulnerable. If in the end we do take the forbidden road, we have a feeling that others brought us to it, that the pressure of our surroundings and of circumstances was so strong that we succumbed.

A very important feature in this story is its evident acceptance of the fact that the situation of temptation is part of human existence itself. Man cannot escape it. It is his weakness. At the same time it is also his strength. Man can make a choice. Pressure of his surroundings and of circumstances plays an important role for good and for evil. Nevertheless, with each choice man demonstrates in his own self his obedience to God, and thus he "makes" his own life.

This aspect is very clearly expressed in Sirach. There in chapter 15, verses 11-20 we read: "Do not say, because of the Lord I left the right way; for he will not do what he hates. Do not say, it was he who led me astray; for he has no need of a sinful man. The Lord hates all abominations, and they are not loved by those who fear him. It was he who created man in the beginning, and he left him in the power of his own inclination. If you will, you can keep the commandments, and to act faithfully in a matter of your own choice. He has placed before you fire and water: stretch out your hand for whichever you wish. Before a man are life and death, and whichever he chooses will be given to him. For great is the wisdom of the Lord; he is mighty in power and sees everything; his eyes are on those who fear him, and he knows every deed of man. He has not commanded any one to be ungodly, and he has not given any one permission to sin."

In this passage, human existence is described as the making of a choice according to one's own understanding and plan. It is God who has determined this mode of existence for man. One of its consequences is that the wrong choice **can** be made; in fact, such a choice often **is** made. Evidently this has always misled people and made them think that God is responsible for the sin: that, finally, sin comes from him. This would mean that God himself causes man to stray from the road which he prescribes. God then would be a deceiver and a seducer; this the author, Sirach, rejects.

The seducer

By whom then is man seduced? Looking back to Genesis 2-3 we must answer: We mislead and seduce one another. One man leads another into temptation. It is Eve who offers Adam the fruit of the forbidden tree and leads him into temptation. One is tempter and seducer of the other. However this is not all. These two people are not the only ones concerned in the temptation. A third party enters, one who stands outside this closed society: the snake. Ordinarily we see in this serpent the

satan, but the text says only "the serpent, more
subtle than any other wild creature that the Lord
God had made" (3:1). The usual interpretation
is based on something we read in Wisdom 2:23-24:
"For God created man for incorruption, and made
him in the image of his own eternity, but through
the devil's envy death entered the world. And those
who belong to his party experience it." This differs
considerably from Gen. 3:1. Even though the snake
was exceptionally sly — the word probably has a
pejorative meaning here — it is nevertheless one of
the wild animals created by Yahweh. When the
serpent is punished (3:14-15) the punishment appears
to be destined for the snake itself. Therefore we
might say that the temptation arises from the milieu
in which man lives. This does not exclude the
possibility that the devil may be active. But he is
not visible nor audible (it is the snake who speaks).
The seducer is hidden behind the snake and the
woman. He himself remains out of sight and manip-
ulates the strings. Scripture tells us that God
himself created both seducers. 3:1 mentions this about
the serpent without emphasis. Of the woman it
says: "The woman whom thou gavest to be with
me, she gave me fruit of the tree, and I ate." It is
not only the test-situation in which man finds himself
(working in the garden in which there is a forbidden
tree) which was willed by God; the seducers, too,
belong to the surroundings God gave to man. We
would be justified in saying that whatever gives the
character of seduction to human existence originates
from God; in any case, it belongs to the milieu which

God gave man in order to enable him to grow into spiritual maturity. It becomes a real temptation or seduction only when we disregard the possibility for good and thus cause the possibility for evil to become so preponderant that we see only this, and begin looking at evil as if it were a good. Never does God make a trial a temptation. This occurs because we ourselves or others direct our attention exclusively toward one aspect of what lies before us.

5

THE TEMPTATION OF JESUS

Repressed thoughts

The temptations of Jesus, mentioned in Holy Scripture for our encouragement and instruction, are seldom used in preaching today. This story of Jesus in the desert (Mt. 4:1-11) ranks with the liturgical lessons; it is read on the first Sunday of Lent. We can safely assume that the priest who has an opportunity to preach about the gospel of that day would usually speak about fasting, and not about the temptations of Jesus.

That these temptations do not figure prominently in preaching is quite understandable. Usually we pay more attention to Jesus' divine nature, and we tend to regard the man in him somewhat onesidedly and exclusively as the form in which God's love for us becomes visible. Seen from this perspective there is a problem: How can Jesus, entirely one with his Father in heaven, be tempted? We fail to see how anything sinful or inimical to God could really have any attraction for him. Perhaps this is one of the reasons why the temptations of the Lord have been relegated to the background of our thinking. This is wrong. There is much evidence to show that

Christians of the first generation found great consolation in the thought that Jesus too was subjected
to temptations and that this reality gave them a
deeper insight into the significance of Jesus' personality. In the letter to the Hebrews we read: "Since
then we have a great high priest who has passed
through the heavens, Jesus, the Son of God, let us
hold fast our confession. For we have not a high
priest who is unable to sympathize with our weaknesses, but one who in every respect has been
tempted as we are, yet without sinning. Let us then
with confidence draw near to the throne of grace,
that we may receive mercy and find grace to help
in time of need" (4:14-16). In this connection we
must mention a little about the temptations of Jesus.

We must take the entire gospel into consideration.
When we speak about Jesus' temptations usually we
have in mind only the story of the temptations in
the desert, extensively described in Mt. 4:1-11 and
Lk. 4:1-13; Mk. 1:12-13 has only a few sentences.
This narrative is important indeed. It would be
incorrect to think that this story — a bit strange
for many faithful readers of the Bible — is the only
place in which we hear about temptations of Jesus.
We may say that Hebrews, quoted above, does not
appear to refer to the incidents of this story at all.
The confrontation of Jesus and the satan, the remarkable transfer to the pinnacle of the temple and
to a high mountain and other details do not lead to
the conclusion that he suffered the very same
temptations which we know. The attitude of the

Lord does not suggest that this enables him to sympathize with our weaknesses. The author of this letter therefore must have had other facts in mind.

Fortunately, we need not rely upon suppositions. The evangelists wrote about other events, from which it is evident that the temptations to which Jesus was subjected came from other people, and that in him too human weakness made itself felt.

Tempted by Peter

We find the most important example of such a temptation in the prophecy about Jesus' passion. Mark and Matthew say: "And Peter took him, and began to rebuke him. But turning and seeing his disciples, he rebuked Peter, and said: Get behind me, satan. For you are not on the side of God, but of satan" (Mk. 8:32-33; Mt. 16:22-23).

This text is very clear. Peter's endeavor to shield Jesus from his passion and death are a temptation for the Lord. Peter is guided by human considerations. Moreover, Jesus shows that this temptation is an attack of the satan himself.

It is evident that this is the kind of temptation which appears more like those which befall us; the evil one does not appear to us bodily. On the contrary, he systematically keeps himself in the background; his activity remains hidden behind certain well intended proposals which others make to us; or he hides behind situations in which we inadvertently find ourselves. This passage shows the real point of these temptations of Jesus: they strive to

make him follow a line of conduct which he knows
is in conflict with what God desires of him. This
resembles our own experience. In Jesus' case this
would mean choosing the road which leads to human
success, rather than the road toward suffering and
death.

Tempted by adversaries

Once we know this we can easily point out other
events in Jesus' life which contained similar temptations. We see scribes and pharisees repeatedly coming
to Jesus to ask him for a sign from heaven (Mk. 8:11;
Mt. 16:1; 12:38). Their intention in making such a
demand — and demand it is, rather than request
— is obvious. They insist that Jesus establish himself as the Messiah by a sign. They wish to see
things with their own eyes. Only after such proof
would they be prepared to believe in him (insofar
as this can still be called "believing"). What they
desire of Jesus therefore is that he adapt himself to
the scheme of Jewish expectations. These to a great
extent are built upon Holy Scripture, the word of
God. But they have been turned and twisted to suit
human possibilities and desires. Adapting himself
to this scheme consequently would have meant that
Jesus allow himself to be led by human considerations and not by God's will, choosing the way of
merely apparent success. Jesus therefore rejects
this demand; he refuses to give this sign.

Did this insistence of the pharisees have the character of a temptation for Jesus? The oldest preaching

of the faith, written down for us in the gospels, saw
it in this way. Whenever such an event is mentioned,
we read that Jesus' adversaries approached in order
to try him, to tempt him, to put him to the test
(Mk. 8:11 par.; 10:2 par.; 12:15 par.; Mt. 22:35; Lk.
10:25; 11:16). The evangelists and the preachers who
had the facts at their disposal obviously considered
these events real temptations: Jesus was being challenged to prove his identity by showing a sign which
would prove him to be the expected Messiah.

For Jesus this might really have been attractive.
Perhaps he was susceptible to the enticements of
visible success. What the pharisees and scribes intended was really to put him to the test, but Jesus
felt it as seduction. Therefore, in answer to the
question whether one should pay taxes to the em-
peror or not, he says: "Why put me to the test?";
this also means: "Why seduce me?" (Mk. 2:15). Here
again we have a case where proposals of other people
constitute a temptation for the Lord.

In the garden of Olives

These texts give no indication of any signs of
weakness or hesitation on the part of Jesus. If
Hebrews did not speak about his sympathizing with
our weaknesses this would not astonish us. Such
weakness in man is the gateway to sin. Where
weakness prevails, sin has already begun. We know
that Jesus is "holy, blameless, unstained, separated
from sinners" (Heb. 7:26). Of course his sinlessness
is not merely the type which we refer to as the
innocence of a child. Jesus can, the same as we,

choose freely between good and evil. For him more than one possibility always lays open. But he always chose the correct way, even when the other was more attractive. The man Jesus subjected himself in love and obedience to the will of his father: he freely chose the road of suffering and death.

Perhaps the oldest preaching understood Jesus' decision to let himself be baptized by John as a consequence of that fundamental choice. By this decision he showed himself to be solidary with sinful man; in principle he undertook to walk the way of sinful man, and to carry the punishment of sin, suffering and death. He purposely chose the way of Isaiah's suffering Servant of Yahweh (52:13; 53:12) who, in place of his people, took suffering and death upon himself. Hebrews connects this choice with Jesus' entrance into the world and puts into his mouth the words of Ps. 40: "When he said above: Thou hast neither desired nor taken pleasure in sacrifices and burnt offerings and sin offerings (these are offered according to the Law), then he added: Lo, I have come to do thy will. He abolishes the first in order to establish the second" (Heb. 10:8-9).

But does all this mean that Jesus' choice was never challenged? Did he only apparently suffer temptations which did not touch him inwardly at all? Did temptation cause any real inner struggle in him? Indeed it did. In the garden of Gethsemane it seems for a moment that we actually see Jesus reeling.

When death stands unavoidably before him, he prays to the Father: "Abba, Father, all things are possible to thee; remove this cup from me; yet not what I will, but what thou wilt" (Mk. 14:36 par.). When he says: "The spirit indeed is willing, but the flesh is weak" (14:38 par.), this holds true also for himself. It was not without reason that "his sweat became like great drops of blood falling down upon the ground" (Lk. 22:44). Although we can only suppose, not really prove, that a successful earthly career held great attraction for Jesus, it is in any case very evident that he met suffering and death with fierce interior resistance. Is not this something like temptation? It is not without reason that he says to his disciples at that very moment: "Watch and pray that you may not enter into temptation" (Mk. 14:38 par.).

Obedience to his Father was for Jesus a matter of course. But it was also a matter of course that he would feel an interior repugnance, and this is why he can sympathize with our weaknesses. Therefore the letter to the Hebrews, evidently alluding to Jesus' prayer in the garden of Olives, writes: "In the days of his flesh, he offered up prayers and supplications, with loud cries and tears, to him who was able to save him from death, and he was heard for his godly fear (variant: only after having drunk the chalice till the bottom); although he was a Son, he learned obedience through what he suffered" (5:7-8). In theory, his obedience may have been a matter of course; in fact, it was something he had to bring to reality by personal effort. And thus he learned obedience.

Until his death

We might think that with this event in the garden Jesus' temptations reached their summit. In reality this was not true. Though the gospels hereafter no longer speak explicitly about temptations, we see them again when Jesus is dying on the cross. I am not speaking now about the nearly desperate prayer of Ps. 22:2: "My God, my God, why hast thou forsaken me?" (Mk. 15:34 par.), which perhaps could also be explained as a temptation, because it sounds as if Jesus' union with his Father was being interrupted at least momentarily. I really mean those who vilified him. These are the same people who had asked him repeatedly — and, we may expect, seriously — to give them a sign which would prove his messiahship. Ironically and sarcastically they say: "He saved others; he cannot save himself. Let the Christ, the King of Israel, come down now from the cross, that we may see and believe" (Mk. 15:31-32). This is the same thing for which they had repeatedly asked: Show us a sign and we shall believe.

Matthew goes further. He expresses the derisive challenge: "If you are the Son of God, come down from the cross" (Mt. 27:40). These words remind us very much of the challenge with which the tempter approached Jesus in the desert, as described in Matthew and Luke: "If you are the Son of God, command these stones to become loaves of bread"

(Mt. 4:3 par.) and "If you are the Son of God, throw
yourself down . . ." (Mt. 4:6 par.). It is improbable
that the first words of the tempter in the desert
should only accidently remind us of the words we
hear under the cross. It seems much more probable
that Matthew chose them purposely to show us how
we should understand this challenge to Jesus.

The gospel of John

In the gospel of John we also read about Jesus'
temptations, even though the words trial, temptation,
seduction are never used. We can point to the
statement which the fourth evangelist· makes in
connection with the miracle of the loaves: "When the
people saw the sign which he had done, they said:
This is indeed the prophet who is to come in the
world! Preceiving then that they were about to
come and take him by force to make him king, Jesus
withdrew again to the hills by himself" (Jn. 6:14-15).
There would seem to have been some who believed
that by this miracle Jesus had given the sign which
they expected. This is also apparent from 7:31: "Yet
many of the people believed in him; they said:
When the Christ appears, will he do more signs
than this man had done?" But not all shared this
opinion. We still hear some clamoring for a sign:
"Then what sign do you do, that we may see, and
believe you? What work do you perform? Our
fathers ate the manna in the wilderness . . ." (6:30-31).
This demand for a sign corresponds to the Jewish
tradition that the Messiah, when he came, would
renew the miracle of the manna. It is also in accord

with what the satan said to Jesus in the desert: "If
you are the Son of God, command these stones to
become loaves of bread" (Mt. 4:3 par.).

Here we may also mention another passage from
the fourth gospel: the one concerning the challenge
of Jesus' brothers: "Now the Jews' feast of Taber-
nacles was at hand. So his brothers said to him:
Leave here and go to Judea, that your disciples may
see the works you are doing. For no man works in
secret if he seeks to be known openly. If you do
these things, show yourself to the world. For even
his brothers did not believe in him" (Jn. 7:2-5). In
this passage it is the evident intention of the brothers
to press Jesus to work some miracle in Judea. It is
remarkable that they are obviously convinced that
he could work such a sign; yet John says they did
not believe in him.

Summing up, we can say that the gospels, atten-
tively read, have a lot to say about Jesus' temptations.
They contain more than one would expect from
reading them quickly and superficially, and they
tell us quite exactly when and how those temptations occurred. It is evident how common and
normal these temptations were. Jesus, like other
people, was usually led into temptation by his
surroundings — in fact by his relatives, his followers
and his adversaries. The main feature of these temptations was what we could, speaking superficially,
call "a question of method." They simply asked
Jesus to act as they expected the Messiah, whom
he pretended to be, to act. From the "Messiah"

they expected a sign by which he would establish himself. They also expected that he would play a political role. However, this placed him in a position where he had to choose between the road of human success and that of human failure, the road of glory and that of humiliation, passion and death. The point was whether Jesus would let himself be guided by the will of his Father or by human considerations. We know which choice he made and how purposely he went his way. But we must also be thankful for the fact that tradition has kept for us some evidence which shows that he sometimes wavered on his road, that he momentarily halted his stride, afraid of what was awaiting him. His flesh too was weak. Hence the author of Hebrews is right in saying that we "have not a high priest who is unable to sympathize with our weaknesses."

The temptations in the desert

Only after these considerations can we open the New Testament and look at the story of Jesus' temptations in the desert, which Mark describes in a few sentences, but which Matthew and Luke tell in much greater detail. The sequence in Luke is very likely a revision of Matthew's description. In this story two things strike us. In the first place it contains many details we already know. In the second place we find a number of things which look very strange.

The method the tempter adopts is familiar to us. He awaits for a favorable situation to approach Jesus, as the scribes and pharisees did. The words he uses are also familiar. He twice begins: "If you are the Son of God," and we hear Jesus replying: "Begone, Satan." The proposal he puts before Jesus is not entirely new either. That he asks him to change stones into bread reminds us of the Jewish expectation that the Messiah would renew the miracle of the manna in the desert; it reminds us also of Jn. 6:14-15 and 6:30-31, quoted above. The challenge to throw himself down from the pinnacle of the temple is, I think, not so much a temptation to what we call presumption; it is connected rather with the sign from heaven for which the scribes and pharisees repeatedly asked. The last temptation (in Luke the second one) shows us exactly what forms the actual background and the real point of all these temptations and challenges: obedience to the Father or to "human considerations" which, as is evident from Mk. 8:32-33 and parallel texts, really are "satan's considerations." It is certainly of importance that the essential features of these three temptations are known to us from other incidents.

Mk. 1:12-13
The Spirit immediately drove him out into the wilderness, and he was in the wilderness forty days, tempted by Satan.

He was with the wild beasts; and the angels ministered to him.

Mt. 4:1-11
Then Jesus was led up by the Spirit into the wilderness to be tempted by the devil.

And he fasted forty days and forty nights, and afterwards he was hungry. And the tempter came and said to him: If you are the Son of God, command these stones to become loaves of bread. But he answered: It is written: **Man shall not live by bread alone, but by every word that proceeds from the mouth of God.**

Then the devil took him to the holy city, and set him on the pinnacle of the temple, and said to him: If you are the Son of God, throw yourself down; for it is written: **He will give his angels charge of you, and: On their hands they will bear you up, lest you strike your foot against a stone.** Jesus said to him: Again it is written: **You shall not tempt the Lord your God.**

Again, the devil took him to a very high mountain, and showed him all the kingdoms of the world and the glory of them; and he said to him: All these I will give to you, if you will fall down and worship me. Then Jesus said to him: Begone, Satan! for it is written: **You shall worship the Lord your God and him only shall you serve.**

Then the devil left him, and behold, angels came and ministered to him.

Lk. 4:1-13
Jesus . . . was led by the Spirit for forty days in the wilderness, tempted by the devil. And he ate nothing in those days; and when they were ended, he was hungry. The devil said to him: If you are the Son of God, command this stone to become bread. And Jesus answered him: It is written: **Man shall not live by bread alone.**

And the devil took him up, and showed him all the kingdoms of the world in a moment of time, and said to him: To you I will give all this authority and their glory; for it has been delivered to me, and I give it to whom I will. If you, then, will worship me, it shall all be yours. And Jesus answered him: It is written: **You shall worship the Lord your God, and him only shall you serve.**

And he took him to Jerusalem, and set him on the pinnacle of the temple, and said to him; If you are the Son of God, throw yourself down from here; for it is written: **He will give his angels charge of you, and On their hands they will bear you up, lest you strike your foot against a stone.** And Jesus answered him: It is said: **You shall not tempt the Lord your God.**

And when the devil had ended every temptation, he departed from him until an opportune time.

The new details are more numerous, but they belong in the margin of the story. The fact that Jesus, according to Mark "was with the wild beasts" (a detail which has never been satisfactorily explained), and the fact that, according to Mark and Matthew angels rendered service to Jesus, are examples. Let us now look at the situation. Jesus' fasting in the desert is not mentioned in any other text of the New Testament. Matthew 11:18-19 gives the impression that Jesus usually does not fast. In Mk. 9:29 we find his statement that some unclean spirits can be driven out only by fasting and prayer. It is the situation in the second and third temptation which is especially strange. According to the story the tempter took Jesus along, first to the holy city, in order to place him there on the pinnacle of the temple and next to a high mountain, where he showed him all the kingdoms of the world. We might solve this difficulty by speaking about visions. This does not seem to be intended in the text. One cannot throw oneself down from a visionary temple. And if the tempter wanted to show Jesus all the kingdoms of the world in a vision, it would not have been necessary to take him to a high mountain. These details, to say the least, are extremely strange, and it is interesting to read old commentaries about them. But let us first of all say that all this lies entirely outside the frame of what happens later in Jesus' life.

Finally a last detail, if we can call it such. In all other cases temptations come from Jesus' surround-

ings, followers, adversaries or brothers, but in this
story of Matthew and Luke the devil himself plays
a prominent role. He disputes with Jesus almost
as would a scribe. We are not told just what it was
that made him recognizable as the satan. The interesting thing is that in the last temptation (which in
Luke has become the second) he exposes himself
so completely that no one would want to have anything to do with his proposals.

Objections

When we ponder over this story of the temptations in the desert, many difficulties come to mind.
The first arises from the situation itself. The triple
temptation is connected with a sojourn of forty days
in the desert, following immediately after Jesus'
baptism in the Jordan. One does not need to be a
thorough scholar to know that this chronology has
its difficulties. The fourth gospel does not mention
this epsiode. Moreover, there seems to be no place
for it. The first chapters of John have several
chronological details which make it impossible that
immediately after his baptism, Jesus should have
gone into the desert to stay for forty days. Whatever we think about this chronology (for it is by no
means certain that John really tries to mention the
events in the sequence in which they happened) at
least we can come to the conclusion that the connection of Jesus' baptism with his sojourn in the
desert was not a point as firmly anchored in the tradition as was the fact of the baptism itself. Otherwise the fourth gospel would not give such a diver-

gent chronology. Therefore we may ask if after his baptism, Jesus really passed forty days in the desert to be tempted by the devil.

The second objection is of a quite different kind, but it leads to the same question: How has anyone been able to learn about the events in the desert? All other temptations took place in public, even though the people present may not have recognized them as such. This is certainly not the case with the desert story. The encounter between Jesus and the satan, according to the narrative, took place without anyone being present. This does not mean that the authors could not have had information about it. This could only originate from Jesus himself. Perhaps he spoke about it to his disciples — for example, on the occasion when he was tempted by Peter, or after his resurrection (cf. Lk. 24:26-28, 44-46).

But we know that the oldest tradition has been very careful regarding the words spoken by the Lord. They tried to preserve them as literally as possible and to hand them down as they had received them — as real statements of Jesus. Therefore, if he had spoken with the disciples about a triple temptation in the desert, it was to be expected that they would have kept his words exactly in the form of a statement of the Lord (as they kept, e.g., a somewhat cryptic pronouncement about the fall of the satan in Lk. 10:18). But nowhere in the tradition do we find any trace of such a record. Even in the story of the temptation itself there is nothing to be found that points to such a tradition. What is contained there as statements of Jesus consists chiefly of certain quotations of Scripture (two of which, Deut. 6:11 and 6:16, are very traditional, because they are taken from the so-called Shema prayer, which every pious Jew prayed everyday). Beyond these words from Scripture Jesus says only: "Begone, Satan," and tradition also uses these words when Peter endeavored to shield Jesus from suffering and death.

It is at least evident from this that we cannot treat the story of Jesus' temptations in the desert in exactly the same way that we treat other passages which explicitly or implicitly speak about temptations of Jesus. The other events took place in public, while here we have an encounter with no one present. The words which Jesus speaks cannot be considered as having the same historical value as those he speaks on other occasions. We can even ask ourselves to what extent they actually can be considered as real pronouncements of Jesus. This means that we must look for a background for this story, a key, which will enable us to see its true meaning. This narrative has a character entirely its own, and no other passage in the four gospels can be compared to it.

Looking for the key

When looking for the key which will admit us to the real meaning of this story, we must for the moment remember what we already know about the other temptations of Jesus. We know with certainty that Jesus could, truly be tempted. This con-

viction also forms the basis of the story of this
desert episode. It bases itself on facts of Jesus' life,
as we have clearly seen in the first part of this
chapter. A second conviction, which plays an important role here, rests on the fact that satan himself
is behind these temptations and that the issue involved was Jesus' obedience to the will of his
Father, which he has to realize by suffering and
dying, and which seems to be avoidable if he allows
himself to be led by human considerations. This
conviction originates from Jesus himself.

Now let us try different keys to see if they fit
the lock. It seems most probable that the best
access will be found in those elements of the story
which suggest that this is not a verbatim report of
an event which took place. One of the circumstances
which — because of the fourth gospel, as mentioned
above — seems doubtful, is the connection between
the baptism of Jesus and his sojourn in the desert
on the one hand and his temptation on the other.
It is important therefore to find out how far this
combination plays a role elsewhere in the catechetical
tradition.

This seems to be the case in the first letter of
Paul to the Corinthians. In the tenth Chapter he
speaks about the temptations to which Christians
are exposed and compares these to the trials of
Israel in the desert after passing through the Red
Sea.

Since Paul explains that this passing through the

Red Sea was a prefiguration of Christian baptism, the circle is complete: after baptism severe temptations follow for the Christian, in the same way that Israel was tempted after its passage through the Red Sea. Christians must take warning from the fall of Israel and remain steadfast. I quote the passage in part. The words in bold are also found, literally or in substance, in the story of the baptism and temptations of Jesus. "I want you to know brethren, that our fathers were all under the cloud, and all passed through the sea, and all were **baptized** into Moses in the cloud and in the sea, and all **ate** the same spiritual food, and all drank the same spiritual drink . . . Nevertheless with most of them God was **not pleased** (compare the words from heaven at Jesus' baptism, Mk. 1:11); for they were overthrown in **the wilderness.** Now these things are warnings for us, not to desire evil as they did. Do not be **idolaters** as some of them were; as it is written: The people sat down to **eat** and drink and rose up to dance . . . Now these things happened to them as a warning, but they were written down for our instruction, upon whom the end of the ages has come. Therefore let any one who thinks that he stands take heed lest he fall. No temptation has overtaken you that is not common to man. God is faithful, and he will not let you be tempted beyond your strength, but with the temptation will also provide the way of escape, that you may be able to **endure** it. Therefore, my beloved, shun the **worship of idols** . . . The **bread** which we break, is it not a participation in the body of Christ? . . . What pa-

gans sacrifice they offer to demons and not to God.
I do not want you to be partners with demons . . ."
(1 Cor. 10:1-7, 11-14, 16, 20).

Here we have one of those fragments of Paul's
letters which is so typical of its author; it reminds
us very much of his rabbinic past. In a manner
which no scribe could surpass, Paul draws a parallel
between the old and the new people of God. He
points out the temptations to which Israel was
subjected in the desert after passing through its
baptism in the Red Sea. In Scripture Israel's vicissitudes were written down for us so that we would
recognize in them our own history. And among
these, baptism and temptations are closely connected,
at least in the Christian-rabbinic interpretation of
Paul.

But is this really the key we are looking for?
Does this parallelism between the vicissitudes of
the old and the new Israel also say something
about Jesus, the Leader of the new people of God,
the new Moses, who fasted for forty days, as Moses
did (cf. Ex. 34:28) when about to proclaim the Law
(the Sermon of the mount in Matthew) and who
really in all respects is our Leader and Savior (Acts
3:15; 5:31; Heb. 12:2)? We need at least an indication that the vicissitudes of Jesus are also connected
with those of Israel.

There are some such indications. The first chapters
of Matthew probably have some traditional material
originating from Christian scribes. According to

these the return of the child Jesus with his parents from Egypt took place in order "to fulfill what the Lord had spoken by the prophet: Out of Egypt have I called my son" (Mt. 2:15). Here we have a text from the prophet Hosea, referring to the liberation of Israel — God's son — from Egypt; this is actually applied to Jesus (cf. **Het Heilig Land,** New Series 12 (1959) 120-122). We may consider this example of exegesis as the "missing link." It cannot be denied that the events of Jesus' life are connected with the history of Israel and especially with the Exodus.

Does the key fit in the lock?

Our question is: Do we have something similar in the story of Jesus' temptations in the desert? In any event, we may be sure that the story — especially as narrated in Matthew — would do credit to an author who has a rabbinic past. The construction of the scene in three subsequent phases, the noticeable climax, the evident connection with certain elements of the Jewish messianic expectations and especially the dispute between Jesus and the tempter, which is exactly like a rabbinical dispute, in which texts from Scripture fly back and forth — all these elements seem to indicate that the author indeed is a former scribe.

It would be very useful if we could find the text from the Old Testament which forms the canvas on which this scene has been depicted. In looking for this text we come first to the quotations dubbed into the story. They are — as far as the answers of Jesus are concerned — all taken from the book

Deuteronomy. Two of them — 6:13 and 6:16 — we need not consider; they are taken from the so-called Shema prayer, which every pious Jew recited every day (and which point therefore to a milieu of Jewish-Christians). They were so commonly known that their presence need not be explained. But this is not the case with Deut. 8:3. This text is taken from a short compendium of Israel's vicissitudes in the desert. If we read the context carefully we find several details which belong also to the decor of the story of Jesus' temptations in the desert: "And you shall remember all the way which the Lord your God has led you these **forty years** in the **wilderness,** that he might humble you, **testing you** (i.e. tempting you) to know what was in your heart, whether you would keep his commandments, or not. And he humbled you and let you **hunger** and **fed you with manna,** which you did not know, nor did your fathers know, that he might make you know that **man does not live by bread alone, but that man lives by everything that proceeds out of the mouth of the Lord.** Your clothing did not wear out upon you, and your foot did not swell, these forty years. Know then in your heart that, as a man disciplines **his son,** the Lord your God disciplined you. So you shall keep the commandments of the Lord your God, by walking in his ways and fearing him" (Deut. 8:2-6).

It is very important that here we rediscover a certain number of details; moreover, the essential features of the situation are clearly indicated. Israel was tried in the desert and punished, as a son is punished by his father, to make it evident if it is prepared to walk in God's ways and obey him. This is also the issue of Jesus' temptations in the desert.

There is however one important difference! Israel is tempted by Yahweh; Jesus is tempted by God's great adversary, the satan. This difference can easily be explained. In the tradition, the conviction that no one but the satan is behind Jesus' temptations is so firm that we cannot relinquish this thought. It originates from Jesus' own conviction. Moreover, the lofty idea of God's fatherly love forbids the thought that a temptation could originate from God himself (Jas. 1:13-14).

An afterthought

If this is the key which fits the lock (indeed, it does not fit too badly) it would mean that we cannot place the story of Jesus' temptations on a parallel with the tradition about the temptations of the Lord in general. This applies not only to the form of the narrative but to its content as well. We cannot consider it a verbatim report about actual events of Jesus' life. It is rather a rabbinic-Christian meditation about Jesus' mission. This is based partly on those traditions about Jesus' temptations which have been kept for us; it may be considered a compendium of these. It is based partially on the Christian exegesis of Holy Scripture (cf. **Het Heilig Land,** New Series, 12 (1959) 120-122). It is an exegesis which still clearly betrays its rabbinic origin; it connects the descriptions of Old Testament events with the facts of

Jesus' life. In a concrete story (which may be considered to be an exegesis of Deut. 8:2-6) we find the conviction expressed that Jesus was tempted by the satan and that he came out of these temptations victorious.

This story is based upon a religious conviction. But this conviction is not hanging in the air; it rests firmly on facts from Jesus' life and on words spoken by Jesus himself. It is a justified and correct conviction. There can be no doubt about this.

Why this narrative is associated with the baptism of Jesus may be explained in two different ways. On the one hand, there is the perspective of the Old Testament and the parallelism of the events accompanying Israel's escape from Egypt and its passing through the Red Sea, which is a prefiguration of baptism. On the other hand it may also be explained by a historical connection between the two events. After the baptism according to the Christian tradition a voice spoke from heaven and declared: "Thou art my beloved Son; with thee I am well pleased" (Mk. 1:11 par.). The story of Jesus' temptation points out to the reader that it befitted this Son above all to be obedient; moreover, that this obedience must make him renounce all human aspirations. He must walk on the road of the Father, a road of human failure.

Whatever was remembered in Christian tradition about Jesus' temptations is brought together here and summarized, and receives a new perspective by being connected to Israel's history. Whatever God began with Israel, he continued and fulfilled in Jesus.

Light from two sides

From this, it would seem clear that in the earliest period of the Church the temptations of Jesus constituted a much discussed topic. They certainly had an established position in catechetical preaching and served a dual purpose.

First of all the fact that Jesus was tempted was a great source of encouragement and consolation for Christians. It is certain that these temptations were frequently used in the so-called "paraenetic" preaching (i.e. in encouraging, exhorting sermons); this is evident from Heb. 4:14-16. No writing of the New Testament so accentuates the glory and majesty of Jesus as does this letter; at the same time no writing so strongly emphasizes the fact that he "had to be made like his brethren in every respect" (Heb. 2:17). This belief that Jesus himself is the exemplar in undergoing temptations helped make them more bearable for Christians. When James writes: "Submit yourselves therefore to God. Resist the devil and he will flee from you" (4:7), he illustrates this with the example of Jesus in the story of his temptations in the desert. And if a preacher wished to speak about Jesus' temptations more extensively, he found very apt material in this narrative. Those who listened understood that Jesus himself had been tempted; but it was also made clear to them how he had withstood the tempter: by submitting to the

will of his Father as expressed in Scripture. Moreover, the great tempter, who prefers to go about in-
cognito, is unmasked here in a very instructive way
inasmuch as the satan himself appears.

There is another reason why the early preaching
spoke about Jesus' temptations. The first task of
this catechesis was to give the faithful a deeper
insight into the question: Who really is Jesus? The
answer was sought in a double approach. First they
tried to penetrate into Jesus' personality by means
of a frontal approach. This means that they gave
information about the facts of Jesus' life and about
the things he had said. The other was an approach
from the rear — by reflection on Holy Scripture
(this means, of course, the Old Testament; the New
was not yet written). This describes extensively the
method of God's dealings with Israel and at the
same time — in a more hidden way — points the
direction in which these are carried out and fulfilled. So the figure of Jesus receives light from two
sides. This is a general procedure in regard to Jesus'
complete person and his entire life (including his
death and resurrection). The same happens with
regard to his temptations. That he was tempted by
Peter and by the scribes and the brethren throws
direct light on this facet of the Lord's person. We
have the effect of indirect lighting in the story of
Jesus' temptations in the desert; this in fact is not
a report of an event, but a kind of commentary
upon Deut. 8:2-6. Here the words of the Old Testament are explained by the temptations of Jesus, and

these in their turn receive a new perspective from this Old Testament background.

This catechetical preaching stresses especially that, for the man Jesus, the fact that he was God's son meant first and foremost obedience, suffering and death, and that this obedience in Christ was by no means unassailed, nor therefore a matter of course.

Theological problems regarding the possibility of a real temptation of Jesus in all this are not taken into account. In the New Testament we do not find texts which show that the faithful of those days were aware of any problems in this regard. The fact that our theology does see these problems should not however be reason to put this reality out of our field of vision. The temptations of Jesus were not sham but realities. Jesus is not simulating. That is why these temptations fully deserve our attention.

6

CHRISTIANS IN TEMPTATION

Freedom from temptations?

Our faith tells us that whatever God did in Jesus serves for our instruction; it also has redemptive value. Whatever the Lord underwent and did transcends the boundaries of his person and finds its echo in those who believe in him. Paul explains this conviction in various ways. He does this by using a certain pattern in his formulas in which contrasts have a central place. Christ, he writes, died for us in order that we should live with him (1 Thess. 5:10). He was born under the Law, in order to redeem those who were under the Law (Gal. 4:4-5). He redeemed us from the curse of the Law, by himself becoming a curse for us (Gal. 3:13). He became poor for us, though he was rich, in order that we should be enriched by his poverty (2 Cor. 8:9). God even made him into sin for us, though he knew no sin, in order that we, through him, should become God's own holiness (2 Cor. 5:21).

Thinking along these same lines, we ourselves could mention a great number of examples, because Jesus really brought about a total reversal, changing

captivity into freedom, darkness into light, guilt
into grace, sin into holiness and death into life, by
entering himself into captivity, darkness, guilt, sin
and death.

Along this line we are inclined to say: He,
against whom temptation could not prevail, became
vulnerable and subject to temptation, in order that
we should be spared temptations. But it is evident
that we cannot reason in this way. Our own experience and Holy Scripture both prove that the
fact that the Lord underwent temptations does not
mean that we are spared temptations. On the contrary, temptation still remains a reality for him who
believes in the Lord and has been baptized. History
repeats itself. Paul sees in temptations, to which a
man is subjected after having passed through the
water of baptism, a repetition of Israel's trials after
passing through the Red Sea and roaming in the
desert. This thought is evidently the basis for 1 Cor.
10:1-13: "I want you to know, brethren, that our
fathers were all under the cloud, and all passed
through the sea, and all were baptized into Moses
in the cloud and in the sea, and all ate the same
spiritual food and all drank the same spiritual drink.
For they drank from the spiritual Rock which followed them, and the Rock was Christ. Nevertheless
with most of them God was not pleased; for **they
were overthrown in the wilderness.** Now these
things are warnings for us, not to desire evil as they
did. Do not be idolaters as some of them were; as
it is written: **The people sat down to eat and drink**

and rose up to dance. We must not indulge in immorality as some of them did, and twenty-three thousand fell in a single day. We must not put the Lord to the test, as some of them did and were destroyed by serpents, nor grumble, as some of them did and were destroyed by the Destroyer. Now these things happened to them as a warning, but they were written down for our instruction, upon whom the end of the ages has come. Therefore let any one who thinks that he stands take heed lest he fall. No temptation has overtaken you that is not common to man. God is faithful, and he will not let you be tempted beyond your strength, but with the temptation will also provide the way of escape, that you may be able to endure it."

Paul seeks to exhort the Christians of Corinth to stand firm in time of temptation. He speaks about this in a very concrete way. The first thing he mentions is idolatry. We need not be astonished that he speaks also about eating and drinking, because the entire chapter deals with the pagan sacrificial meals. The exhortation not to commit fornication certainly was proper in a port like Corinth, a city which in this regard had a bad reputation all over the world. Still, the background of all these exhortations is the conviction that a Christian is subject to temptations as much as the fathers in the desert.

This passage would be sufficient to convince us that temptation is a real situation in the life of a Christian, just as it was for the Israelites; it is truly connected with human existence. Every man must find his own way and in so doing he continually arrives at crucial points where he must make a choice. This is true for a Christian too.

The seducer

Considering the evolution which took place within the Old Testament, we might expect that the New Testament would no longer speak of temptation in connection with God himself. The element of enticement and seduction gradually came to the fore in regard to temptation — so much so that we no longer see God in it. We are preoccupied with the negative elements of the wrong road which lies open and to which the seducer points, that we see temptation entirely as the work of the satan. In 1 Cor. 7:5 Paul warns married Christians to be careful if they desire to deny themselves (and therefore also one another) marital intercourse "lest Satan tempt you through lack of self-control." The situation Paul describes here is in itself of such a nature that it could easily induce a man to unfaithfulness. Yet Paul seems to feel the need to bring satan into the picture. It appears as if satan continually lies in wait to do his worst, whenever the occasion offers. Or, as Peter says (1 Pet. 5:8), he "prowls around like a roaring lion, seeking some one to devour." Hence it is not at all strange that Paul here calls satan "the seducer," as if this were his proper name (1 Thess. 3:5) and as if he were personally involved in every temptation.

A very remarkable text in this regard is Lk. 22:31-32. Here we read the words of the Lord:

"Simon, Simon, behold, satan demanded to have you, that he might sift you like wheat, but I have prayed for you that your faith may not fail; and when you have turned again, strengthen your brethren." It seems as if the same situation is present here as is described in the introduction to the book of Job, where a heavenly satan obtains permission from God to bring Job into the most terrible situations in order to test his faith. These conditions are so conducive to unfaithfulness that they approximate the character of absolute seductions. The role of God in such cases must be restricted to permitting the temptation (1 Cor. 10:13).

The evil day

There is one period in which it appears more difficult than ever to "stand against the wiles of the devil" (Eph. 6:11). That is "the evil day" (Eph. 6:13), which begins at the end of time. Then comes "the hour of trial which is coming on the whole world, to try those who dwell upon the earth" (Rev. 3:10). For before the "ancient serpent, who is called the devil and satan, the deceiver of the whole world" (Rev. 12:9) will be conquered, he will be allowed — so it seems — to do his worst. The thirteenth chapter of Revelations is a symbolic description of the manner in which this great deception and seduction will take place. The author makes use of a language filled with mysterious images, just as Paul did when he wrote to the Christians of Thessalonica. They must not let themselves be shaken in mind as if the day of the Lord has come. "That day will not come, unless the rebellion comes first, and the man of lawlessness is revealed, the son of perdition, **who opposes and exalts himself against every so-called god** or object of worship, so that he takes his seat in the temple of God, **proclaiming himself to be God** . . . The coming of the lawless one by the activity of satan will be with all power and with pretended signs and wonders, and with all wicked deception . . ." (2 Thess. 2:3-10). We find these same expectations clearly expressed in the gospels, though in other terms: "Take heed that no one leads you astray. Many will come in my name, saying: I am he! and they will lead many astray" (Mk. 13:5-6; cf. Lk. 21:8; Mt. 24:23-28). These direct attempts to seduce the faithful will moreover be accompanied by persecutions and other calamities, which will lend special force to the seductions. This is a power indeed so satanic that it is not possible to associate it with God, except to ask him: "And lead us not into temptation, but deliver us from evil" (Mt. 6:13; Lk. 11:4).

Struggle hardens

When temptation is so severe that it appears as seduction, a provisory conclusion presents itself as expressed in the letter of James: "Let no one say when he is tempted: I am tempted by God; for God cannot be tempted with evil and he himself tempts no one" (1:13). When the temptation can no longer be considered a test-situation giving man an opportunity to realize his possibilities for good as well as for evil, but when it rather is seduction to sin, God

can have no part in it. It is striking however that
the author of this letter also sees a positive side
in this temptation when he writes: "Count it all joy,
my brethren, when you meet various trials, for you
know that the testing of your faith produces stead-
fastness" (1:2-3; cf. Rom. 5:3-5). But in saying this
he no longer sees temptation primarily in the perspective of an activity of satan. Rather he focuses
attention on what happens within man himself: on
those things which respond to temptation: "Each
person is tempted when he is lured and enticed by
his own desire" (1:14). And when he writes: "Blessed
is the man who endures trial, for when he has stood
the test he will receive the crown of life which God
has promised to those who love him" (1:12), it is
evident that he puts together some opinions about
temptation which have little to do with a specifically
Christian perspective. These are pronouncements
about human nature in general: they retain their
value for a Christian, but do not reach him where
he is entirely and formally Christian.

Liberation from temptation

Although a Christian does not meet less temptations than a non-Christian (rather, more!), nevertheless a new perspective is open for a Christian, which
completely alters his situation.

There are the unavoidable temptations connected
with the conditions in which we live. This is briefly
summarized in 2 Pet. 2:9: "The Lord knows how to
rescue the godly from the trial." These temptations
are temporary, passing, connected with the actual

situation of Christianity, with the earthly phase of the Church. But in spite of the present temptations — or, more accurately, because of them — our lives tend toward a future of glory, where there will be no more temptations.

This point has been elaborated in Christian tradition by way of a number of contrasts like those quoted in the beginning of this chapter. We find them in 1 Pet. 4:12-13 (the first part of this is very difficult to translate): "Beloved, do not be surprised at the fiery ordeal which comes upon you to prove you, as though something strange were happening to you. But rejoice insofar as you share Christ's sufferings, that you may also rejoice and be glad when his glory is revealed." This is more distinctly and extensively elaborated in the first chapter of the same letter: "Blessed be the God and the Father of our Lord Jesus Christ! By his great mercy we have been born anew to a living hope through the resurrection of Jesus Christ from the dead, and to an inheritance which is imperishable, undefiled, and unfading, kept in heaven for you, who by God's power are guarded through faith for a salvation ready to be revealed in the last time. In this you rejoice, though now for a little while you may have to suffer various trials, so that the genuineness of your faith, more precious than gold which though perishable is tested by fire, may redound to praise and glory and honor at the revelation of Jesus Christ" (1:3-7).

Consequently the Lord will really deliver us **from**

temptation. This means that in order to be delivered from them we must first pass through them: that we are delivered **in** the trials (which consist of what we usually call temptations, or persecutions or contumely). This is what the Lord himself says. For this we may turn again to the gospel of Luke, of which chapter 22 is for the greater part dedicated to temptations. We read here about Jesus' own temptation in the garden of Olives where he, subject to a heavy temptation — remarkably enough — says to his disciples: "Pray that you may not enter into temptation" (22:40, 46; in verses 47-53 and in 54-62 we see Peter succumbing twice!) It is in this very same chapter that Luke combines another doctrine with instructions about service, the special hallmark of the true disciple (22:24-27): "You are those who have continued with me in my trials; as my Father appointed a kingdom for me, so do I appoint for you that you may eat and drink at my table in my kingdom, and sit on thrones judging the twelve tribes of Israel." Solidarity with Jesus in **his** trials and temptations is the road to participation in his glory. But we might add at once: This solidarity brings with it a concomitant fact that the followers of the Lord **themselves** will also be subjected to severe trials and temptations.

This gives us reason enough to rectify the incorrect contrast which we met in the beginning of this chapter: Jesus, against whom temptations could not prevail, became vulnerable and subjected to temptations on our behalf, in order that he might

liberate us from temptation. But this does not mean
that he keeps us free from them. By taking upon
himself our sins, sufferings and death he did not
set us free from these things. So also he does not
set us free from temptation. We will be liberated
from them, but first we have to pass through them.

Not alone

This is not all. Even though it is only later that
we will be liberated from temptation, this does not
mean that the Lord leaves us alone in the trial. He
does save us from temptations; but he also protects
us while we are in them: "Because you have kept
my word of patient endurance, I will keep you from
the hour of trial which is coming on the whole world,
to try those who dwell upon the earth" (Rev. 3:10).

This is what the author of the letter to the Hebrews has in mind when he writes: "Since then we
have a great high priest who has passed through
the heavens, Jesus, the Son of God, let us hold fast
our confession. For we have not a high priest who
is unable to sympathize with our weaknesses, but
one who in every respect has been tempted as we
are, yet without sinning. Let us then with confidence draw near to the throne of grace, that we
may receive mercy and find grace to help in time
of need" (4:14-16). The Lord is at our side. He
never leaves us alone — not in our weaknesses, nor
when we reel (cf. about Jesus reeling 5:7-10). He
has experienced all this himself: "Since therefore
the children (we, his brethren, are these children)
share in flesh and blood, he himself likewise partook

of the same nature, that through death he might destroy him who has the power of death, that is, the devil, and deliver all those who fear of death were subject to lifelong bondage. For surely it is not with angels that he is concerned but with the descendants of Abraham. Therefore he had to be made like his brethren in every respect, so that he might become a merciful and faithful high priest in the service of God, to make expiation for the sins of the people. For because he himself has suffered and been tempted, he is able to help those who are tempted" (2:14-18).

Certainly, not every one finds courage in the thought that the Lord assists us in temptations, as if he knows this entirely from his own experience. It is necessary to have lived for a time with this conviction and with faith before he can fully realize what it means.

CONCLUSION

Looking back

We have now reached the end of the journey through the texts in which the Bible speaks about people in temptation. We can now bring this book to a close. But we will add a short chapter in conclusion, because some readers may feel a need to allow the various impressions received during this journey to settle in their minds. Sometimes, even these are contradictory. The meaning of the word "to tempt" has undergone a considerable change along the way. It has almost reversed itself: presently it is interpreted as "to seduce" rather than, as originally, "to try." This is all the more important insofar as the identity of the "tempter" has also changed.

What are we to do now? Is it sufficient to duly accept the information that the oldest books of the Old Testament saw the "trial" as coming from God himself? No; this is exactly what appeals to us more today than the later conviction that we must look for the devil beneath every temptation.

Is it possible then to reconcile these two different ways of considering the same reality? It is and it is very easy. To establish some sort of brief summary may be helpful. We must bear in mind that the different aspects, though based on an indivisible experience, are nevertheless of a different nature. Thus we might make a distinction between what we ourselves experience and what we know from revelation — remembering that this distinction is certainly not correct in all respects.

What experience tells us

Experience tells us that temptation exists: we ourselves experience a definite urge to do something which we know — clearly or vaguely — to be wrong. In this urge two factors usually combine. There is more or less heavy pressure from outside (the snake in the garden of Eden, Peter when he wishes to shield Jesus from suffering, the pharisees and the scribes who ask Jesus for a sign, the persecutions a religious man has to bear). But this pressure, which engages the tempted man almost entirely can become really dangerous only if man has a weak spot, where he is not able to withstand the pressure and where the allurement may have fatal consequences. Therefore the letter of James can say — though in a somewhat one-sided and exaggerated way —: "Each person is tempted when he is lured and enticed by his own desire" (Jas. 1:14). Without such a weak spot, temptation has no chance of success; yet we feel that the real and decisive factor generally is the pressure brought to bear by other people, or critical situations and circumstances. It is for this reason that Genesis 3 highlights the role of the snake and this is the reason why stress is purposely put on the fact that Peter, the brethren and the adversaries of the Lord brought pressure to bear upon Jesus.

Another factor — as real as the first — about which experience tells us — is the human reaction: the resistance. This may take place in different ways, or may not take place at all. In Gen. 3 man does not resist at all. He succumbs at once to the pressure the woman brings to bear upon him. In the woman however we notice a certain definite resistance. She no longer sees the forbidden fruit as it really is; she looks at God's veto as being much bigger than it is. Such forced resistance does not make man endure. He overdoes it. The force he exercises is too great. For this reason he loses his equilibrium and falls. Success can be assured only when there is a well-balanced resistance. We have an example of this in Job. When everything he has is taken from him he concentrates entirely on confidence in God. We see the same with Jesus too. He reels in the garden of Olives, when all pressure is put upon his weak spot: his fear of suffering and death. But he also keeps in mind the one thing which is all important: the will of the Father, which must be fulfilled at any cost. He reels, but does not fall.

We will not discuss the other tempters, God and satan. They are not part of the human empirical world, but stand outside it. This was also the case (it may be useful to make this remark here) in the time covered by the Old and the New Testament.

Looking at the text it may occasionally seem otherwise. But it only seems so. In such cases the facts
of revelation have found a resonance in faith; this
faith has acquired such an echo in Holy Scripture
that the insight of the believer and human experience
seem to coincide. What we experience here is a
dual reality become one: the reality of faith and of
empirical knowledge.

Revelation and religious reflection

Non-empiric realities can be classfied under revelation, and religious reflection on revelation. These
are two different realities. In revelation we have
God speaking in a recognizable way. This is not
the case in our religious reflection. This is rather
a rumination on God's message. But the Spirit of
God is also active in this meditation — in a different
way, however. Both ways have this in common: they
constitute for us the totality of divine revelation. It
seems to the author of this book — but the reader
may of course hold a different opinion — that it is
better to consider the text about which we have
spoken as the result of (inspired!) reflection on facts
of experience and certain data from revelation. They
are not in themselves real data of revelation in which
God's speech is immediately recognizable.

In summarizing this religious reflection we should
pay attention to God and the satan. Only one who
believes can assume that God and the satan play
a role in the trials of man. But they do not play
a role **outside** the empirical reality of temptation
itself. If satan tries to seduce man to sin, this does

not mean that he exercises influence **in addition to**
other seducing factors in the situation. He does not
stand beside them, but he works through them.
We must say the same about God. When we state
that God tries man, we must not picture this as if
he did this independently of the trials and seductions which life brings. In some way he works in
these. It is understandable that the Old Testament
originally ascribed trial especially (and perhaps exclusively) to God; it is also natural, because attention
is then paid only to the fact that temptation is an
existential situation. This is a very important insight
of faith. In the beginning this thought seems to have
gone hand in hand with another — less correct —
opinion, that God brings man, and especially his
elect, into a test-situation to learn something about
men. It is evident that this is much too human
representation of God. If he brings man into temptation, he does this only to give him the opportunity
to actuate his choice for God in a crisis and to
allow him to realize his union with God from within
himself. In such a temptation good and evil stand
beside one another as two invitations, only one of
which may be accepted.

Only when we see trials as a seduction (when all
stress is put upon the attractiveness of evil) God's
adversary must get an active role. This is evidently
the case when someone wishes to seduce us to
something which we clearly see as wrong (remember
Peter who is called satan!). In such a case the situation is no longer experienced as a double possibility.

Therefore it is not accidental that, especially in temptations which come to us from our fellow men, we experience a satanic influence, while we see diffi- cult situations as coming from God. The story of the fall in Gen. 2-3 is a clear case in point. The situation in the garden surrounding the forbidden tree is ascribed to God; pressure from the serpent has something satanic in it.

In the temptation of Jesus, revelation and experi- ence are identical. Perhaps we could say that this experience is a revelation for us. In his experience it is revealed to us that temptation is truly connected with human existence, something we cannot escape. For him besides his experience there is also religious insight. In the light of his relation to the Father he sees and understands his experience and can unmask and withstand the seducer.

When Paul in 1 Cor. 15 connects the temptations of the Christian with those of the old Israel, this is not so much real revelation as religious reflection. We can say the same of Matthew 4 and Luke 4, where Jesus' insight into his own experiences, in a concrete description, places satan in personal opposi- tion to him. We can say the same too about the encouragement which the writer of the letter to the Hebrews distills from this scene.

Likewise, temptation is for the Christian himself a matter of experience, upon which light is thrown in many ways by revelation and religious reflection.

He may look at it as a task which God imposes upon him, which gives him the opportunity to prove his promise of faith. He may also see this as an attack of satan who desires to alienate him from God and who wishes to rupture his basic endowment as man. He may find strength in the fact that in these temptations the Lord stands beside him as one who has overcome the same temptations, but only after he had experienced his own weakness under the pressure of trial. Finally he knows — not from experience, but from faith! — that the Lord will save him from the temptation.

God or the satan?

But even after this summary, in which all the facts have been compared and placed in their respective positions, the question still stands: Does my trial come from God or from the satan? Of course we **can** answer: from both! But this is an answer which originates from religious thinking rather than from religious experience. When we begin with the latter, the conviction will sometimes prevail that it is God who tries us; at other times we will be convinced that it is the satan who assails us. This will also depend upon our personal attitude: Do we feel fear and uncertainty when confronted by the menace? Or are we primarily concerned with the possibility of actualizing, with God's help, our faith in him by actually opting for him? Now we might think that the aspect which gradually becomes stronger in the books of the Bible, — the satanical aspect — should also be prevalent in our own lives. This would mean that we should especially accentuate the satanic character of temptation.

It seems entirely correct, nevertheless, to give the other thought a more prominent place in the way we look at life. Why? Because nervous resistance is a one-sided attitude, which prevents us from seeing everything in its proper proportion (cf. Gen. 3:3). A positive attitude is much more reasonable. This does not mean that we are allowed to seek the so-called proximate occasion to sin. But where this occasion is unavoidable — and it becomes more and more unavoidable since we Christians again live in a diaspora — we should remember that such an occasion is also a proximate opportunity for showing ourselves, with God's grace, faithful to our word.

Finally, a defensive attitude does not agree well with us today. One who looks at the temptations of his life as coming from satan is driven to the defensive. When we look at them as test situations willed by God, we not only get out of our defensive position, but we gradually will cease thinking in terms of struggle and fight. We will see life much more vividly as an actualization of the possibilities which God has provided, as the fulfillment of our ever changing tasks. Of course, this is too one-sided a viewpoint. But who could have the illusion that he is free of such one-sidedness? Our attitude, positive in its direction is more in keeping with our present situation.